THE RIGHT THING

Also by C. K. Stead:

Poetry

Whether the Will is Free
Crossing the Bar
Quesada
Walking Westward
Geographies
Poems of a Decade
Paris
Between
Voices
Straw into Gold: Poems New and Selected

Fiction

Smith's Dream
Five for the Symbol
All Visitors Ashore
The Death of the Body
Sister Hollywood
The End of the Century at the End of the World
The Singing Whakapapa
Villa Vittoria
The Blind Blonde with Candles in her Hair

Criticism

The New Poetic: Yeats to Eliot
In the Glass Case: Essays on New Zealand Literature
Pound Yeats Eliot and the Modernist Movement
Answering to the Language

Edited

World's Classics New Zealand Short Stories
Measure for Measure, a Casebook
Letters & Journals of Katherine Mansfield
Collected Stories of Maurice Duggan
The Faber Book of South Pacific Stories
Werner Forman's New Zealand

C. K. STEAD

The Right Thing

AUCKLAND UNIVERSITY PRESS

ACKNOWLEDGEMENTS

Poems in this collection have appeared in the following:
(United Kingdom) *London Magazine, London Review of Books,
New Writing 7, PN Review, Poetry Review, Times Literary Supplement*;
(New Zealand) *Landfall, Listener, New Zealand Books, Salt, Sport*;
(Australia) *Sydney Morning Herald*; (Canada) *Malahat Review*;
(United States) *Cumberland Poetry Review*. 'Encounters' was written
for the 70th birthday celebration volume, *Paeans for Peter Porter*.

My special thanks to the President and Fellows of St John's College, Oxford, for
kindness and hospitality during my tenure as
Senior Visiting Fellow, 1996–7.

First published 2000

Auckland University Press
University of Auckland
Private Bag 92019
Auckland
New Zealand
http://www.auckland.ac.nz/aup

© C. K. Stead, 2000

ISBN 1 86940 221 9

Publication is assisted by creative nz
ARTS COUNCIL OF NEW ZEALAND TOI AOTEAROA

This book is copyright. Apart from fair dealing for the purpose of
private study, research, criticism or review, as permitted under the Copyright
Act, no part may be reproduced by any process without
prior permission of the publisher.

Cover design by Christine Hansen
Printed by Astra Print, Wellington

Contents

The Right Thing	1
Good Morning	2
Janet Frame's House	3
Ars Poetica	5
An Ode to It	10
Les Enfants du Paradis	11
Ode to a Nightingale	12
Mercredi-Gras	13
John Cage at Harvard, 1988	15
Xanadu	17
Reservation	20
Cartoons	21
September, Perigord	29
Likenesses	31
Running in Oxford	32
The Keys of the Kingdom	33
Loyalty and Booze	34
Exit	35
Suffenia the Poet	37
Ravidus the Bookman	38
Easter 1916	40
Shelley	41
The Other Place	43

Horace III, 30	45
Revisiting Bristol	46
The Sparrow	48
The Universe	50
Fame & Companion	53
Lessons in Modern History (i)	54
Lessons in Modern History (ii)	56
Absence	59
Zagreb	60
Hollywood	61
Even Newer English Bible	64
Notes from 'A Natural Setting on the Far Side of the World'	65
Play it Again	69
Nine Nines	72
Encounters	76
Crete	78
Stories	88
Horatian	91

The Right Thing

'Have you cracked
the snowfall's code
or the language of light?

'How much honey
do the Pleiades hold?
Where is Orion unclasped?

'What is the weight
of shadow
on a hardened heart?

'How do the ten
standing orders of heaven
differ from sleep?'

'I am a sod, Lord'
Job answered correctly.
'I can answer nothing.'

Sheep were his reward,
good pasture and camels,
also daughters

and the defeat of foes –
Eliphaz the Temanite
and Bildad and Zophar.

Good Morning

To greet
after a night of frost
the oldest of the gods
alight in the mangroves
walking on water
clearing the air
all the way to the blue hills
best to behave as if
several inquisitive centuries
with their books and banks of knowledge
had passed you by.

Time is now
now is for ever
and the god is risen.

Innocent
ignorant
enjoy his hands on your face.

Janet Frame's House

There's a pool table
she plans to exchange
for a desk
of the same size.

At the back are pines
and a tidal creek
with mangroves
and crabs.

Downstream
from the racecourse
a traffic bridge
rushes and whispers.

Needled grass
under the pines
remembers
summer picnics.

At full tide she says
if she had a dinghy
she could row across
for the shopping.

Indoors again
I take down a cue
from its wall-clip
and pot the black.

I too would like
such a vast desk
but secretly wish
she would keep the table.

Ars Poetica

i

Barefoot in shallows
                      his sleeves
trousers
sodden
                      the small boy
talks to the tide
              to the water-birds
to the tall sky
                and the Bay's
furthest reaches

                  If your words
                    could speak
his world . . .

ii

would it be enough?

        Was it Yeats who said
poems must be packed in salt?

iii

     The birds are
migrating somewhere

     They pause here
to feed and to quarrel
and the nights
    are full of their noise

iv

     Recipe for poetry
(or Spanish omelette) –

       potatoes
      green peppers
       deep oil
in a heavy pan

eggs beaten lightly
     cooked slowly

eaten cold
with white wine

v

Centre-table
the potted cyclamen
                  responds to
'Reach for the skies . . .'
                        or
'All in favour please raise . . .'

Its five eager hands
                  in white gloves
on thin stems
      catch light from the window

vi

                  The birds stand
each on one leg
                    in a wind
that ruffles and nudges

                  They don't topple
                        but hop –
the favoured leg
asleep in its feathers

vii

Vice-verse
arse-verse

                        the poem as
                        scatalogical
                        or obscene
artefact

is more than
                  cocks and cunts
                  twats and dicks
or the rhyming of bum   with come

                  It is Martial
Catullus

              the Roman realists

testing
testing

viii

              The four-year-old
lost in a crowd
fists in eyes
                and wracked
with sobs –

              this is apocalypse
the poem at the end of the world

ix

The wind has died
                and the moon
        will not settle the question

              It lies on the water
                  mimicking itself
in a French accent

              'Alfred de Musset'
                  it reminds me
'died young'

                      and

'Where is your blue guitar?'

x

Persistence
                of the child's
rainbow and rose
                  but a glory
(Wordsworth)
gone from the earth

An Ode to It

Clergyman Spooner
praised his wife's
cunning stunt.

His was
la langue anglaise
the common tongue.

He knew
the English languish
for lack of lip.

There should be
(he argued)
an ode to it.

To what?

Yes!

Les Enfants du Paradis

Garance! Garance!
Come back!
She rides on in her coach.

This is the final scene.
The mime-artist
jostled by the Mardi-gras crowd
is losing her for ever.

The villain
with his villainous moustache
the contemptuous Count
the brave thespian –
each has loved her
after his fashion.

It's the mime-artist she loves
and he loves her
but Fate has determined . . .
(and so on).

Garance
with your round eyes
and your beautiful smile . . .

Garance!

ODE TO A NIGHTINGALE

When one joked
she laughed
when the other
danced with her
she crooned in his ear
songs about booze
and forest murmurs
and flowers-in-the-nose
unseen in the dark.

At her door
she kissed them both
first one
who laughed again
then the other
who experienced
a moment of blackout
kiss kiss
goodbye
to comrades in arms
veterans
of magic casements.

Mercredi-Gras

What stays with me most
of that Edmonton winter
is the bitterness of wind
on the High-Level Bridge
and the whiteness of snow
on the ice of the river.

The bus drivers struck
and I walked to my office
wearing ear-muffs under my hat
pyjamas under my clothes
thinking about Wittgenstein
as I checked off the days.

Far below
skiers threaded among trees
down to frozen water
while an orange sun-ball
too sluggish to lift itself far
hugged its pillows.

Wittgenstein was troubled
because it seemed to him
Wednesday was fat
and Tuesday lean –
not as we say that meat
is fat or lean
nor as he and his landlady
were respectively

lean and fat –
it was more (he reasoned)
a question of usage.

But the particularity
of his sense of it
the sleekness of Tuesday
and especially
the grossness of Wednesday
troubled him in the night.

Indifferent in Edmonton
Tuesdays and Wednesdays
came and went.
The bus strike ended
but even at twenty below
I went on walking
inside my pyjamas
Wittgenstein beside me
in that ear-biting wind.

John Cage at Harvard, 1988

Sonorous
he reads into a mike
a text he means should be
devoid of meaning.

In the semi-circle
of the wooden theatre
we're respectful
of his fame.

A handout explains
the trouble he has taken
to achieve
a random text.

'To have so tinged'
he intones
'my Soviet sudden change . . .'
He gives it light and shade.

Feeling floors and walls
begin to melt and slide
I cling to grammar
and to fact.

A student
scrabbles in her bag
to silence a radio
turned on by his talk.

Under a young man's legs
in the front row
an unscheduled dog
shakes itself.

Xanadu

(to Helen Vendler)

Drying dishes with
the teatowel
you bought me at the

Kennedy Centre
depicting (faded now)
Boston's

first church and
the ride of Paul Revere,
I remembered

a Harvard dinner
when jointly we
offended a

Catholic and a
Jew by insisting
there was no God;

recalled our
obstructing traffic
on the steps of the

Casino at Monte
Carlo while we
teased out the

'pastoral
eglantine' of the Keats
ode, and Shakespeare's

'vagabond flag upon
a stream'; and a
year later

together at Sligo's
White Swan Hotel
watching the

rush of waters
seaward from the Lake
of Innisfree.

How make a locked
box for the lady
famous for keys?

How cook for one
whose sure taste will
locate the secret

ingredient?
Rationalists, yet for whom
poems bespeak

a First World,
what's common
between us is open to

public view. No
secrets – only perhaps
a hint that

once, in a parallel
life, lissome
in Xanadu,

we may have danced
away our innocence
and the night.

RESERVATION

      I hope you got that stuff
                     about the Navaho
did you Gretchen
like your own Maori
          a highly spiritual people
              those pottery beads
for example
and that leather thing
            they meant something
also the way they stepped here
and stepped there
and stepped here again
               did you notice
to the drum-beat
             woggle woggle
                jim jim
tittle tattle
whatever.

         My goddam camera's
jammed Calvin
            how about you
               Mary-Anne
for Christsake
         what are we here for
didn't anyone get a shot?

Cartoons

8.8.96

Scientists discover
there's been life on Mars
though dead for aeons,
that's to say yonks.

President Bill says
if there's life in space
he wants the United States
to have an input.

Somewhere in Siberia
a bronze statue of Lenin
falls over
and kills a man.

Watch out for the dead!
They leave their traces –
ideas for example
and heavy statues.

12.8.96

A lost tribe is found
in the Manokwari
jungle region
of Irian Jaya.

Pale-skinned and timid
when spoken to
they hide
behind trees.

Mornings they gather
food in the forest
afternoons
they fish their lake.

Maybe they sing
at evening
omba omba
the reports don't say.

Their sentinels
are green parrots
taught to screech
when strangers approach.

13.8.96

Today it's revealed
that ex-Prime Minister
Paul Keating
kept a trampoline

in his back garden
and bounced on it
daily
to ward off cancer.

At the weightless
apogee
of each bounce
he believed

was the nanosecond
when bang!
the malignant cells
were expelled.

26.8.96

Alzheimered
Ronald Reagan
no longer remembers
he was the world's

most powerful man
carrying in a flat case
the codes
to corpse a planet.

All forgetful
he knows however
that Nancy
is his mother.

So why
after his haircut
does she lock him
in his room?

When the big light
goes down
he sits at his window
in pyjamas

hearing the moon
mumble to the hills
its threats
and rumours.

21.9.96

A Catholic Bishop
runs off with
a Mrs MacPhee
and sells his story

to the popular press
but the cash is to go
to his teenage son
by a former mistress.

His housekeeper
who used to browse
in his wastepaper basket
says there were others.

Everyone's distressed.
The ailing Pope,
the nervous clergy,
the sad parishioners

of Argyll and the Isles –
even (I think)
I am distressed.
How could it be

we ask one another.
Isn't a hand job
good enough
for the modern priest?

29.9.96

In this state
the dead man rules.
All bow at morning
to the figure in bronze,

all sing at evening
the late leader's song.
Here is the Future
as the Past saw it

and it doesn't work.
In the countryside
peasants and workers
inherit the earth

which is barren.
Evening television
offers 'ten tasty tips
for cooking grass'.

30.9.96

Faber and Faber
the beautiful woman
among publishers
has a stalker.

A disgruntled author
he threatens
by phone and fax
to slash her tyres

and smash her face
if she won't oblige.
It's rumoured
her biggest boyfriends

Hughes, Heaney, Harold
Pinter, and the like
are taking turns
to see her safely home.

1.11.96

After two centuries
of displeasure
Horsham will acknowledge
its famous son.

A sculpture
honouring Shelley,
poet, atheist
and adroit eloper

will be unveiled
in the town square.
Three thousand
gingerbread men

each with a fact-sheet
about his life
have been distributed
to local schools.

25.3.97

Thirty-nine men
in black trousers
and new Nikes
have packed their bags

taken drink and drugs
put their heads in plastic
and stretched out
under purple sheets.

They're off to join
a space-ship travelling
behind the comet
Hale-Bopp.

'Goodbye
hard world
so much less
than the heart desired

'we've had enough
of your impure
inequitable
website ways.'

Everyone's dead
but look –
the packed bags
all left behind!

Who can be held
responsible?
Such an oversight
at the moment of glory!

Up there
trekking behind Hale-Bopp
they're quarrelling
over a change of clothes.

SEPTEMBER, PERIGORD

Walking to the village
to buy our breakfast baguette
she grazes on the small black
vineyard grapes.

Returning
she picks six apples
from trees that skirt
the millhouse drive.

She will stew them
with peaches and plums
and the bowl of blackberries
from roadside ditches.

After pasta and salad
to eat them out of doors
with *fromage blanc*
and the local wine

under the silent wing
of bat and owl
is a kind of grace –
thank you to the gods

or our lucky stars.
A grandchild
cries in the night
and she lies awake

listening to the stream
discourse to the millrace
on gallic themes –
how enjoyment

can be gratitude
made manifest;
how luck and good order
are the twins of fortune.

Likenesses

(to Craig Raine)

Hegel seems to me to be always wanting to say that things which look different are really the same. Whereas my interest is in showing that things which look the same are really different. – Wittgenstein

King of Comparison, clever as the Reverend Moon
you marry a dozen thises to a dozen thats

in a flash of light, while I admire and demur.
Nothing, for example, is so like a swallow

as these swallows are, describing their twittering arcs
without analogy, in and out of an archway

that opens on a village square. Under umbrellas
we sit out on the cobbles with cool drinks, eating

a sandwich of crudités made for us in the bar.
Under the arch roof we can see the mud-fixed nests

like inverted igloos, or those domed African huts
on a stone landscape yellow and pitted like the moon.

Siesta time. The swallows have a silence to fill
and the stones for echo. They are the bats of the day

as bats are the swallows of darkness. There's no end
to likeness it seems, only because nothing is the same.

Running in Oxford

You might have done this
forty years ago
loose limbed
and two stone lighter.

To wrench
from its fabled lodges
ordinary 'Oxford'
and make it real –

would that have been
a life's work
worthy
as any other?

No answer!
A snaking spray
practises
its signature

on the greens,
the famous spires
make their points
over the heads

of autumn trees,
and look –
an elderly visitor
is running in Oxford.

The Keys of the Kingdom

(for John Kelly)

'This is the Late Key – use it only
when the porter's lodge is shut.
It opens the small wooden gate in the wall
on the St Giles side.
This mortice lets you into the College Library
(at night, remember, you may see the ghost of Laud).
This other opens the carpark gates,
and also the iron gate to the gardens
from Canterbury Quad (the one
Wilde remarks on, though he wasn't
of course a St John's man).
And this – this is the V2.
It lets you into the Senior Common Room,
the Xerox room, the Japanese garden,
the North Quadrangle by the door from the carpark,
and also the gardens by the back gate
through the wall from Parks Road.
If all else fails, remember
try the V2 –
it will seldom let you down.'

Loyalty and Booze

Over dessert he sank low beside me
seeming in his cups to slip under the board
so that he eyed his glass directly
and it stared back at him, a woman
perhaps, dangerous and much desired.

Around they went and around –
the port wearing about its neck
on a chain a medal declaring it was PORT,
followed closely by the florid claret,
the sweet wine, urine yellow,
and a silver snuff-box.

We'd come from High Table to this panelled room
a dozen gathered over the dessert
to celebrate his birthday.

'Your friend', he murmured of one recently dead
'was an officer. By that I mean he was loyal.'
Loyal to what? I wondered
since all the talk had turned
on his manifest failings.

'Drink was what did for him,' my companion declared
allowing the port to pass.

EXIT

At sixty Cicero
you'd resolved your silence
would sound a lament
for the lost dignity
of better times
but the ravens came
that day we brought you ashore
roosted in your rigging
beat on your windows
followed when your servants
(fearing such omens)
carried you to a wood
where your death was waiting.

It's said you pushed
your head out of the litter
to afford your assassins
a cleaner strike.

Death, Velleius declares
in his farewell oration,
has taken from you
only pains and griefs
and made your glory greater.
Against the tyrant, he says
your name stands for ever.

We nod and murmur
graveside concurrence
but truthfully, friend,
if the choice had been yours
old age in the shadows
or this glorious death
which would it have been?

SUFFENIA THE POET

Cleopatra, Helen and the Mother of God
are some of her roles, but also I think Cassandra
truth-teller, deeply regretful, painfully honest
as she reads her lying verses in a lying-down voice
a neck-scarf hiding her wattles, and that painted-on face
the one, she thinks, that launched a thousand ships
but more likely sank them, smiling in the lectern light
saying over and above the words, 'Believe me! Believe!'

Ravidus the Bookman

Don't forget, Catullus
how that porker Ravidus
after his crisis
of lung and liver
(brought on he said
by the stress of a merger)
bounced right back,
left his job
as prince of publishers
to be literary editor
of a quality broadsheet
where he behaved
much as before
seldom reading books
(others did that) –
it was more a matter
of sniffing the wind
giving ear to gossip
having an eye for fashion
a feel for the market
and only now and then
hacking out a column
of consensus bookchat
in his execrable prose.

A hack is a hack is a
hack, says Cornelius
and I suppose he's right
but whenever did a Grub Street
penny-a-liner
sit above the clouds
in a comfortable chair
with a drink and headphones
doing the *Times* crossword
wondering where the hostess
with the lovely legs
spent her nights in New York –
and all on the profits
of other men's sweat?

Believe me, Cornelius
when lungs and liver
at last send Ravidus wailing
through streets of the city
down to where the dead men
write forever unpublished,
those who bought him drinks
will piss on his name,
those who were indifferent
will forget it,
and another and another
and another Ravidus
will press and elbow forward
to fill his chair.

EASTER 1916

*(for Seamus Heaney
to whom I gave the book)*

Irish Thomas MacDonagh
thirty years ago
in this Oxford bookshop
I found your poems
published by Hodges Figgis
Dublin, 1910.

Songs of Myself you called them –
how lovingly
you must have turned
those long-ago pages
dreaming of fame
and your country free.

Alas Thomas MacDonagh
shot by the British
it's not your poems live on
in the mind of Ireland.
It's your dying,
your death.

Shelley

1 *Viareggio, 1822*

So long in the water
the face half-gone
but in the pocket
the identifying book –
Hunt's copy of Keats

and on a finger
the ring he'd ordered
to be inscribed
'*il buon tempo arriva*' –
the good time will come.

So now, on an iron frame
over a driftwood fire
with salt and incense and wine
the brain of a poet
boils in its skull.

Unable to watch
Byron swims to his yacht
a mile offshore.
Hunt waits in their carriage
parked in shade.

When the rib-cage
bursts open
Trelawney tears out
what he thinks is the heart
burning his hand.

Afterwards
Hunt dines with Byron
and they drive like madmen
through the Pisan woods
singing and shouting.

2 *Oxford, 1996*

Left of the porter's lodge
past the music room
on staircase three
of the College that expelled him
he lies now on his side

naked in white marble
under a domed sky
painted with stars,
his poet's head pillowed
on a poet's hair,

his penis pointing
earthward,
his blind eyes turned
towards the white
radiance of eternity.

The Other Place

We were talking about gender.
Not gender as it occurs in the popular mouth
meaning sex. This was grammatical gender
and how, even in the Germanic languages
where you'd expect concurrence
nothing is dependable.
A feminine noun in German
may be masculine in Danish,
and so on. Then there was the question
of the sounds of Dutch
so unfamiliar to the Anglophone ear
when the written forms are so close.
An ordinary chat over lunch, you see,
into which I threw, at a pertinent moment,
a forty-five-year-old memory from a textbook,
Jesperson's *History of the Language*,
scoring a small point.
It was then the blow-fly, very large, very black,
and very loud, began to buzz
my chicken salad. I waved at it
gently at first, then vigorously,
but with little effect. It persisted,
unfairly I thought, because to my left
was another chicken salad,
opposite were kidneys – there were, in fact,
no end of lunches appetizing to a fly,
but it would have none of them.
And nobody spoke of it.
While I went on waving, the talk,

tenacious as my winged tormentor,
moved on to the politics
of calling the sagas Old Norse
or simply Icelandic.
I should, I suppose, have swatted it
and asked the butler to remove the corpse
but I lack the style,
or call it the habit of command –
and that, I believe, was its point.
Even the flies here
can recognize a stranger.

HORACE III, 30

Drunk with pleasure
at what had flowed from his pen
the poet dashed off a letter
to Melpomene.

Greater than the pyramids,
proof against the worst
the north wind could throw,
his thirty odes, he told her
would outlast bronze.

He would die, yes
but what she'd given him
would defeat the goddess of Death.
Accordingly he demanded
Apollo's laurel.

Was the Muse offended?
Not for a moment!
He was the vehicle only.
The honour he was claiming
she saw at once
was meant for her.

Felicitations, Horace!
There's no euphoria
and no frankness
like those of a mind unchained
finding wings in words.

Revisiting Bristol

(for Kay)

Here's the street lamp
our first car
a grey Ford Popular

was parked under,
and windows we
looked out from afraid

to drive, wishing
it would vanish in the
pea soup. Back

after ten cars and
four decades
it's as if our black-

and-white snapshots
didn't lie. The colours
must have been

our supplement of
youth. The Senecas,
father and

sons, and grandson
Lucan, were Cordobans
addicted

to Rome. One came
and went; one stayed
and triumphed; one fell

foul of mad Nero
and bled in his bath.
Would they have

bridled to be called
colonials? Like birds
on some

needless but
habitual migration
we've crossed skies

and crossed them
as our 'opposite isles'
chased each other

never to meet.
So what's belonging
unless it's to

one another
and to our own
history, the books which

made us what we are,
and those that will
tell our story?

The Sparrow

Hymenaeus
when Catullus called you forth
from Helicon Hill
promising to praise you
above all the gods
you were to wear (he instructed)
a scarlet cloak
and yellow shoes
and with flowers in your hair
carrying a torch of pinewood
you were to dance like a demon.

Son of Urania
all this no doubt you deserved
but was it wise
to give to powerful Venus
such cause for envy?

I saw you this morning
busy among leaves
under the apple tree
your eye bright
your movements quick
your commonplace plumage
unruffled in the autumn sun.

Like Catullus
you'd dispensed with
the scarlet gown
the shoes and the garland.
The whiff of woodsmoke
was not of your making.
Like Catullus
you were hard at work.
Like him
you'd survived.

The Universe

i Cogito ergo sum

He moves
not like winged Mercury
nor Venus rising from the sea
but on wheels.

He speaks
not with the tongues
of men and of angels
nor a zephyr among poplars
but with the voice of a robot.

He thinks
not as you and I think
interrupted by lusts and compassion
but like a computer.

Ordinary mortals
oil his wheels
feed him
and replace the batteries
in his voice box.

'There may be a God,' he quacks
imagining a brain like his own
but as large as a planet.

ii Poetics

Wild as
water on a hot-plate
a summer ant
flicked off its trail
an antigen
confronted by T-cells
here is a single atom
aurum
dropped on glass.

Things fly apart
that want to be together,
things are forced together
that want to be apart.

'Conductivity'? Yes.
'Lymphocytes'? For sure!

But where are the words for
the pain and the panic
the escape and the joy
the I and the thou?

iii Lost in space

'How will I find it?'
asked Gabriel
sent Earthward
to bespeak a Virgin.

God told him, 'Go past
the Park of Cubes.
Just short of Chaos
find the Region of
the Self-Igniting
Spheres-in-Flight.

'Ignore the fires
and the blinding light.

'Find the Blue One.
Strike there.'

Fame & Companion

The young man on the door, reading her novel,
asks her to inscribe it. Around the pool table

in a smoky bar, the artists, stringy-grey haired,
are caricatures. We wait in a smokeless parlour

till her table's ready in the dining room.
Curtains are drawn on the garden. Eyes are on her

as we settle to talk. She wants to begin a novel
but the year's been wasted, she says, on promotion tours

that drove her close to breakdown. Ah that such
deserved good fortune should fall on such frail shoulders,

I want to mock, but it seems her distress is real.
Her work today was a review – nine hundred words

for nine hundred pounds. Mine was ten lines for nix.
It felt (I tell her bravely) like a state of grace.

LESSONS IN MODERN HISTORY (i)

1956 West

Anagram
ants
    even in Eden
        need
honey so
spooner-like
        he
hied to the louse
and she
    (his Eve) said
        it was as if
sewers
    were flowing
        frew
  'er sitteen room
    at numbah
ten.

1956 East

Mr B and
    Mr K
is there a tiger
in your well-hung-
arian tank?

```
                    No
but there's a
                 buda-
pesky student
         under it.
```

Lessons in Modern History (ii)

1 C.K.

Castro and Cuba
Kennedy and Krushchev
the Cs and the Ks
were strong that year
and so was fear.

That was 1962
when only the C and the K
preceded by an L and a U
got us through.

2 1963 – HiJKL

Oh but leave out the Ks
we should have known
it was the Js and the Ls
that mattered –

Jack and Jackie
and what Lee
did for Lyndon
and what the other Jack
did to Lee
also (you could say)
for Lyndon.

There's symmetry for you –
History on first-name
terms with itself!

3 1965

was when
                              (for Death)

a line on a map
became
                              (for Death)

an international
boundary
and a zone
                              (for Death)

a sovereign
state.

4 *1968 made*

a bullet for Bobby
a martyr of Martin
of Tet an Offensive
of Lyndon a loser.

5 1974

Broken by a break-in
tangled in his own tapes
it's goodbye again
to Tricky Dicky
Cold Warrior
and Comeback Kid
who was going to end the war
with more bombs
and fewer boys.

6 1975

It ends in panic.
It ends in helicopters
shuttling to ships offshore.
It ends when a single tank
laden with flags and flowers
and peasant soldiers
bursts through the gates
of the President's palace.
It ends (don't say it)
in defeat.
It ends in the timely divorce
of Mars and America.

ABSENCE

Have you left at last, my Clodia?
Catullus hunts for you upstairs and down

from room to room through the empty house;
looks for you in the leaf-strewn garden

where the squirrel wars with the magpie.
In books, in memory, in the mysterious rattle

of language where he so often found you,
he searches without success. This winter morning

is windless, cloudless, and a low-angled sun
drives its shafts blindly up the Woodstock Road.

But you on whom he waited, on whom he depended –
you're gone, leaving him nothing but a silence.

O.K., but you know he'll wait by the broken gate
under the beech tree at evening, and in the night

when the house creaks, he'll listen for your return
never expecting it, never giving up hope.

Zagreb

There were four in the café,
the poet
and three women
(a perfect world!) –

Jadranka
who asked the questions
Ljiljana
who translated them
and Kay
his second self.

So much intelligence
and so much beauty
trained on the one who must answer –
how could he do other
than shine like a star?

Out in the countryside
even the terrible war
held its breath.

HOLLYWOOD

(for Roger Donaldson)

In winter sun
we lunch by the pool
in a garden

of oranges and lemons
palms and olives
where the

chill of desert shadow
signals
snow in the mountains.

Spring, you tell me
will flower purple
in the courtyard

and in high summer
only the drift
of mists up from

the Pacific
will temper hot winds
down from the hills.

All day with our script
we play the game of
put and take

each 'say we do
this' sending me back
to the keyboard

to the mysteries
of 'slug line', 'cut to'
'action', 'fade'.

Evenings
we watch classic movies
suggesting 'say we dos'

for tomorrow.
My novel's shrinking
under our hands

into scene-and-speak
the rest dropping away
like ripe

olives on the path
to your front door.
Last night I dreamed

those giant letters
high in the hills
spelled GOLLYWOG

and the tall palms
running seaward on Sunset
were fountains.

'Will our movie be made?'
I asked the ocean
and heard

clear beyond wave-break
the budget
whistle in its cage.

Even Newer English Bible

The Lord is my caregiver so I'm O.K.
He suggests I put my feet up
or take a stroll down at the Bay.

That way, He says,
you keep out of trouble.

I have one fractured rib
and three more cracked or bruised
from a dive off the stairs –
but the ambulance came
and the hospital staff
they comforted me.

I eat out
where my reviewers can see me.
Someone puts pasta on the table
with basil and cheese
and a bottle of red.
Someone promises me a massage.

This could go on for ever!
Who needs to win Lotto?
God, I'm so lucky!

Notes from 'A Natural Setting on the Far Side of the World'

        I've been reading a poem
'New Zealand outback'
           by Lee Harwood (b. 1939)
of Brighton, Sussex,
        author, my *Who's Who* tells me
of *Wish You Were Here*
        and veteran of marriages
with Jenny Goodgame
        and Judith Walker.

It doesn't seem he's ever
        set foot in our space
nor is his poem about
        the New Zealand 'outback'
(something we don't have).
        Rather it addresses
a certain 'Marian'
        who wrote him a poem 'about
a lily and . . . love'.

        So it's an adult
and sultry afternoon
        and there's an open book
on the table in his poem
        given him it seems
by 'Marian', and showing
        his long-lost forebear
snapped with two others in
        the New Zealand 'outback'.

          Mario Soldati (b. 1906)
                    ends *The Orange Envelope*
          sending his narrator,
                    a writer called 'Carlo'
          to live in 'Auckland, New Zealand'
                    where he looks from a window
          at 'tall kauri pines,
                    palm trees and giant ferns'
          all in a 'meadow'.

                    Three years ago
          on the Ligurian coast
                    my friend Bacigalupo
          thought I should meet
                    his friend Soldati –
          but the novelist, 89,
                    no longer remembered
          what in his novel was 'true'
                    and what he'd invented.

          He must, he felt sure
                    though an age ago
          before Alzheimer's began
                    to cloud the picture
          and lose the plot
                    have been ashore at
          'Auckland, New Zealand'
                    at least in his mind.
          Where else did travel occur?

       But now, darkening
almost to blackness
     here's *Premeditated Murder*
by Belgrade Croatian
       Slobodan Selenic (b. 1933)
in which the narrator
        distressed at her lover's
return to the war-zone
        refuses to kiss him

or say goodbye
      and consumed with remorse
at word of his death
       tramps the battlefield
with an old man
       until they find the corpse
faceless, half-buried
       with its jet-black hair
and delicate hands

       to be kissed too late
brought home in a box
       on the top of a bus –
and on the last page
       asked by friends
'What will you do?'
     'I'm going to New Zealand.'
'How long?' they ask.
      She tells them, 'For ever.'

Enough of fictions
                           here's the morning paper
20 May 1997
                           photograph front page
of Alenka Vlaj
                           no date of birth but
glamorous in jeans
                           personal secretary to
Prime Minister Drnosek

                           of independent Slovenia
with Tone Koscak
                           Prime Minister's bodyguard
bare feet in water at
                           Tucks Bay, Coromandel
with their new-born son
                           delivered on the beach
by Fern Drysdale
                           a local midwife

because Alenka wanted
                           the birth to happen
'in a natural setting on
                           the far side of the world'.
Is this a case of
                           life imitating art
or the wide-bodied jet
                           making remoteness easy?
They fly home Friday.

Play it Again

(for Les Murray on his 60th Birthday, 17.10.98)

Corporate raider
in the larder
of language

with more than a tyre
to spare
and girth to go

he lacks the classic
pose of restraint
his motto

'Never say When'
his poems pack-horses
unloaded

line by line
under a blazing sky
or in the

downpour that speaks
in gutters and spouts
of Excess.

Here the Golden
Disobedience
is practised.

Here the Dark Celt
meets Anglo-Oz. Here
the Fat Boy

cries in a cave
for his Mother
and tries to grow

into the shape
of a woman.
Here the Poor Cow

finds words to match
its beautiful eyes
and takes heart.

Here the Coolongolook
stops
to reflect and the

Jindyworobak
finds itself
sophisticate.

None-the-Les Murray
now that the Black Dog
is gone

this day brings you to
a number
cheerfully round.

Nouns will be busy
at being
verbs at doing

down the long road
where gums flap
their bark bandages

at a rush of galahs
and the world
(your reader)

urges you
in the glint of webs
and the scents of

morning
to go to your desk
and play it again.

Nine Nines

America

Not its railtracks and freeways – they go through it.
Not its great cities – they hide it behind their eyes.
Not the small towns – they tell us only stories
of what it once was. Not Rocky Mountains, and not
the red-rock canyons where John Wayne whacked the Apache.
Oval Office, Pentagon, cookies, cute freckled children,
Blacks singing blues – these are not America.
America is a continent hidden in a broken promise.
It lives in a word. Think of it. America!

Moon

One daughter had borrowed the other daughter's shirt.
There was a stain wouldn't come out. After the row
he sat outside in the dark and smoked just one
forbidden fag that made his heart thump harder.
Ti-tree and toe-toe pushed their spikes and feathers
into a skudding sky. Briefly the moon sailed out –
now a veiled disk, now a pale and furrowed brow.
It didn't say, 'Don't take these matters to heart,'
or 'Life is conflict.' The moon's great virtue is silence.

Sylvia

Ten days after he was, you were born.
Heading out past sixty he's still hanging on

but you baled out at thirty telling the world
'Dying is an art. I do it exceptionally well.'
Now you're a young poet of deserved fame,
he an aging one, forgetting reputation.
From where he sits cool Daddy looks at you.
He sees the pain, and the brat, and the brat in pain.
Living is an art. He does it as well as he can.

Zen

Must poems have always the extravagance
of Death or Love? Nine lives might not be enough
even for the cat sleeping in this almost silence
of a distant handsaw's panting. Blue sky, green trees,
white weatherboards, a garden full of washing
all arms and legs, cram full the breathless moment.
Nothing to be gained by running at it headlong.
Answer the Master. Tell him what the World saw
when a thrush flew down from the pear tree.

Miroslav Holub in Toronto, 1981

His passport feared the man from the Embassy
at the back of the hall. One word out of place
could cost it a life. Scientist Holub professed
to no opinions. As poet, he was cleverly arcane.
On his last day we bought umbrellas together
and stood in a glass cage with a girl with red hair
pelted by flowers of rain. How could he know
the trump had already sounded for Jericho?
His passport-faced goodbyes implied for ever.

Oxford, 1997

That was no ordinary season – both rivers frozen,
also the canal, and the fountain outside the Radcliffe
forming a curtain around its man of bronze
who held a platelike shell which day by day
the god of winter heaped higher with frozen snow.
Ducks went walking on water. Swans caught napping
were closed upon. The world had become its own
white wedding cake, or a virgin, holding her breath,
conjuring behind her veil the turbulence of green.

Night Sequiturs

At 4 a.m. remembering reading Frost at midnight
and thinking of 'Frost at Midnight' by S.T.C.
put me in mind of that shark with its fin de siècle
languidly cutting warm shadow in Hobson Bay
south of the pipe in bright blue autumn weather
promising cool nights. It was Paavo Nurmi of Finland
and later Murray Halberg used to run round and around
the track at the same pace steady as the second hand
of a second-hand stop-watch going, not counting the sheep.

Brunel – Bristol 1830

First build four stone ramparts, then fire an arrow
dragging a fine thread, the thread to draw a cord,
the cord a light rope, the light rope a heavier,
and so on, until the heaviest, aided by a winch,
will drag across the valley the bulk of one chain.

This action repeated twice times 33
puts something where nothing was – 66 chains
on which to suspend your bridge. It's there still.
The weight of modern traffic hangs by a thread.

St John's College Library

Fading, sensitive to light, the pencilled head
of the king who lost it hangs under ruffs of curtain.
His son, a king restored, once asked the College
if he might have it. In return, he assured them,
he would give whatever in reason was asked of him.
Can a Sovereign's wish be refused? Gravely the dons
present him with his father's depicted head.
And what in return, he asks, do they ask of him?
'Sire,' they answer, 'our wish is to have it back.'

ENCOUNTERS

(for Peter Porter on his 70th birthday, 16.2.99)

i (Sydney)

I had the Chair but
he was the one
who professed.

Small talk
was never less
than interrogation.

His big flinty specs
strip-searched my mind
for reasons.

I was arrested
for a coolness
re Schubert

and the heroic couplet
of Alexander
Pope.

No bleating about
the bush,
this was Les Murray's

Athenian copper
back home where
the heart was not.

ii (London)

Dick Whittington
at home in his head
up the long

Paddington stair
from fabled streets
paved with paper

he's listening for
the dinkum oil
the ring of gold –

Peter the rock,
Porter the carrier,
the burden

no more than knowledge,
the object
no less than art.

CRETE

1 *Hania*

I wrote that swallows
are the bats of day
as bats are
the swallows of darkness
but here they are at dusk
the bats up early
swallows working late
over and through a roofless ruin
made by German bombs –
as you might watch
in the undersea half-light
of Suda Bay
fish cruising or stalled
in the split and sunken tonnage.

2 *May 1941*

Poland France Belgium Holland
Yugoslavia mainland Greece
all these had fallen
and with fewer German deaths
than in the first three days
of the battle for Crete.

Something had begun to go wrong.

3 *The Memory in Stones*

Three small and perfect
sea-crafted pebbles
I took from Maleme Beach
one mottled grey
one bauxite red
and one a dazzle
of white and whiter –
but the red
bled on my hand
stained what it touched
and I left it behind.

4 *Hill 107*

Who commanded the hill
commanded the airfield –
who commanded the airfield
commanded the island.

It's a graveyard now
(Soldatenfriedhof) –
four-thousand-something
dead young Germans
claim each his piece
of Crete for ever
in the name of the Reich.

5 Zen

Rough clad
facing forward
he stands in his skiff
and with quick light stabs
of blades in water
guides it slowly over
the almost glass
of the morning harbour
looking ahead and down
left, then right
then left again.

From my balcony
on the second floor
of the Hotel Lucia
with a matching patience
I watch and wait.

6 E.C.

Venice built the sea wall
Turkey the mosque
modern Greece the hotels.

Time made the ruins
with German assistance.

7 He Learned . . .

That the entrance
of the bearers of death
can be beautiful
as a season of flowers
opening all at once
across a field of sky.

That the underworld
of the olives
is its own place
of red earth
and green lizards.

That wild daisies
can be midnight blue
and that the Anzac poppy
blooms also in Crete.

That birds will sing
between bomb blasts.

8 In the Clearing

'Face to face
at fifteen paces
both surprised –
he in grey with his rifle
I in khaki with mine.

'Hit the deck?
Fire from the hip?

'I waved him away.
It was an impulse
as if to say
"There's no need . . ."

'He grinned
waved back
and was gone
among the olives.'

    9 Headstones, Suda Bay

The last parade is forever
and the drill perfect.
Pale-faced in the sun
rank on rank unflinching
they out-stare
the Aegean blue
and a white ship at anchor.

British
        Australians
New Zealanders
each with name and rank
or the inscription
 'A soldier of
  the 1939–1945
    War
  Known unto God.'

10 *Veterans, 1998*

Climbing the hill
into Galatas village
for the commemoration
I trudge behind them
the tall RAF man
and the little brown Kiwi
Mr Edwards from Thames.

'Your lot pulled out
before it really got started'
says Mr Edwards.

'Ay,' says the other.
'But by that time
we'd only one plane left
and a third of us were dead.'

11 *Minoan*

These stones you see
of an irregular wall
yellow-orange
below the level of the street
where the church was bombed –
they're Minoan.

What does it mean
Minoan?
It means old.
No.   Older than that.
Before they started the clocks.
Ancient.   Oldest.
Minoan.

12 *Blitzkrieg*

It must be their speed
gets these giant ants over
the hot sand and stones
on Maleme Beach –
each ant-foot's touch
a microsecond.

Shelled with heavy pebbles
they survive even
what appear to be
direct hits.

13 *Fear?*

'I'd lived with it
– or call it anxiety –
all my twenty-one years.

'It was a relief, really
having something
to be afraid of.'

14 At the Villa Andromeda

These are career soldiers.
Their weapons are formidable
but they'll never use them.

Brass and bellows.

These are the diplomats.
Here's a famous hostess
and an admiral of the fleet.

Wind and water.

These moustaches belong
to local politicos
eager for advantage.

Subtitles superfluous.

Here are the plates and glasses
on tables pool-side
under tragic stars.

Food for reflection.

The dirge is for lost lives –
or is it for a glory gone
beyond reach for ever?

Anthems and flags.

15 *Hotel Lucia*

Morning light
strikes up off water
and the shutters
make lines of it –
a glittering
         flickering
handwritten message
from HQ –
untranslatable

the writing on the wall.

16 *The Bayonet*

'. . . hiding in a well
or behind it.
He fired at our backs.

'"Get him," the major shouted.
"Get the bastard."

'If I'd shot him
there would have been a bang
and silence.

'Half a century
he's been quiet on the hill.
Half a century
I've lived with the scream.'

17 Last Post, Suda Bay

Should we disturb you
my dead compatriots
so well placed here?

Should we disturb ourselves?

Your silence is absolute
unless we pretend
it's you who speak in the wind.

Not forgotten
but unfathomable.

More vivid than yesterday
and like yesterday
gone beyond call.

Stories

(to A. S. Byatt)

Bright children
alert to the Dark
and what it might mean

like to be told
a story, and some
grow up to be

themselves tellers of
tales. Today
driving from Uzès

I found the gorge road
closed by slips
and was forced upward

into the mountains.
Now we've swum
in your pool and walked

to the local *auberge*
and you tell,
as dark comes down,

your tale of one
who wished to write
a Biographer's

biography,
and how you made up
all the names of

your characters
from the elm tree
and its predators –

Sir Elmer Bole,
Phineas G. Nanson,
Scholes Destry-Scholes

who join us
at our table outdoors
while the near hills

listening
loom nearer, and the spirit
of ancient

France, wary as always
but attentive to
la langue

anglaise,
holds its vast breath
or sighs along the roadway

and in the branches
over our heads.
Twenty-one years

since we began
this game of giving
and receiving

and still we play it,
as by the firelight
in caves and

flame-lit farms
invention must once have run
stride for stride

with probability its
partner
holding at bay,

but only while the breath
lasts and the last
word remains

unsaid,
the bat-winged person
who must come to the door.

HORATION

The days they run, they run
keeping the score on our faces,
Licinius, and Death
with his fluoride teeth
and famous, boring torso
must always win.

We who've lived
paying our dues to the sun
on a fruitful isthmus
between two harbours –
what can we offer as bribe
to that dry-eyed skuller
on the darkest river?

What use that we escaped
war, and the worst of weathers?
Soon his sporty Lordship
will beat us to our knees.
The last lips
will have been kissed,
the last race run,
and in our cellars
the best bottles
will belong to another.

Together then
Licinius
let's practise it bravely –
saying goodbye
and meaning for ever.